Rob Roy Mac

Rogue or Romantic Hero?

by Gilbert J. Summers

The Macgregors' motto, 'S Rioghail mo Dhream' (Royal is my Race), reflects their ancient origins and their descent from the Siol Alpin – the original Caledonian natives who opposed the Romans in the Battle of Mons Graupius in AD 84. Finghin, Abbot of Glendochart in west Perthshire in 966, was the founder of the Clan Gregor. He was reputedly the grandson of Gregor, son of Dungall who reigned over the Picts and Scots from 878 to 884. Gregor had reached the throne by slaying Kenneth MacAlpine's youngest son Hugh. This is the Royal line mentioned in the motto, linking the tenth century founding of the clan with its even more ancient origins.

The Macgregors' territories reached their greatest extent in the thirteenth century, though through their refusal to hold their lands by any means other than the sword, they were gradually deprived of them, especially by the Campbells. By the sixteenth century they were landless and maintaining themselves by raiding their neighbours. This policy in turn led to severe Acts of Proscription from 1603 to 1633 intended to destroy the Mac-

Glen Gyle at the head of Loch Katrine – Rob Roy's birthplace.

Loch Lomond – its southern edge in the lowlands and northern reaches in wild country – had on its eastern borders the Macgregor territories of Craigrostan.

gregors. Yet, so insecure were the fortunes of the crowned heads of the Commonwealth in the mid seventeenth century, that even the Macgregors came into a measure of favour as supporters of the Royal House. The Acts against them were not enforced for a time, although later in the life of Rob Roy they were to be reinvoked. Thus at the time of Rob's birth in 1671 the branch of the family from which his immediate ancestors came was living in Glen Gyle, at the head of Loch Katrine in the Trossachs.

Lieutenant-Colonel Donald Glas, Rob Roy's father, gained his title for services in the army of King Charles II, the Stuart King on the throne when Rob was born. The supporters of the Royal House of Stuart were known as 'Jacobites' and thus from his father Rob would have developed Jacobite sympathies from an early age. However, the Stuart dynasty was drawing to a close. King James II (VII of Scotland) took the throne in 1685 but within three years anti-Catholic feeling and complex political in-fighting had resulted in the downfall of the last of

the Stuarts. King William and the House of Hanover were now to rule both England and Scotland.

The Hanoverians, usually in the form of Government troops, were to be Rob's enemies much later in his career but in the last decade of the seventeenth century these adventures lay in the future. In Glen Gyle the young Rob Roy was growing up with only peaceful intentions.

If political events were to shape the life of Rob Roy, then geographical circumstances were also to prove of importance. The Macgregor territory around Loch Katrine was close to the rich farmlands of the south, which spread out around the southern edge of Loch Lomond. To the north of the Macgregor territory, the country was even wilder, with the high peaks of the Breadalbane Hills concealing many secure places where men could outwit the Lowland forces of law and order with comparative ease.

In the whole Highland area, since written records began, cattle had played an important part in the economy. By the

With Highlanders regarding cattle as communal property, cattle lifting was widespread, particularly in times of hardship.

numbers of his cattle, a chieftain's wealth would be measured. Rent to a feudal superior would be paid with them. Not only were they currency, but an important food source – almost, in fact, a kind of 'Welfare State' on the hoof, to be used in time of need. And part of the economy was also based on the sale of these cattle in the Lowlands. This meant the moving of huge numbers of the beasts each autumn to places like Crieff which had an annual cattle market or 'tryst'. Cattle-droving was a much-valued skill throughout the Highlands, requiring knowledge of terrain and weather as well as business sense – in short, cattle-dealing in all its aspects was risky but potentially profitable. The cattle business was to be Rob's choice.

However, there was more to cattle-dealing than buying, fattening for market and selling. In those wild and lawless times, cattle were regularly spirited away from their rightful owners by any of a number of clans – the Highland code of morality excluded cattle when it came to theft, regarding them as communal property. Therefore the Macgregors took their share in times of hardship. And clearly, if cattle were at risk from marauders, then protection could easily be provided – at a price. Thus the Scots word 'mail' meaning rent, became 'blackmail' and referred to tribute paid to ensure protection of the cattle. This convenient revenue-earning business, which the Macgregors themselves operated, had official sanction from the Government of the day and led to the forming of properly organised squads, known as 'Watches'. No Highlander would have been troubled by the odd double standard of stealing cattle when the occasion arose while protecting the property of others.

The young Rob Roy would not only receive training in the skills of the community – everything from ploughing to boat-building – but he would also be trained in weaponry. It was the custom for the Highlander to carry weapons from the age of sixteen, following early training with a stout stick as a substitute sword. Many writers have commented on

This modern statue by Benno Schotz in Stirling emphasises Rob Roy's long arms!

Rob grew into early manhood, these survival skills were ready to be put to the test.

A suitable opportunity presented itself when Rob was still in his teens. A party of MacRaes from Kintail had entered the territory of the Earl of Breadalbane at the west end of Loch Tay and stolen fifteen cattle. The services of Rob Roy and his men were requested by the Earl himself. As they formed the official Watch, it became their responsibility to track down the missing stock. From Breadalbane's Finlarig Castle – nowadays an ivy-covered ruin – the band set off northwards. Soon they were upon the wastes of Rannoch Moor and by the second day, deep into the mountains of Badenoch. This was hostile country, held by the MacPhersons. But as night fell, Rob saw firelight flickering ahead. His reconnaissance revealed a band of gipsies who told his party that the MacRaes were only a short distance away. With a surprise attack at dawn that drew blood from both sides, Rob and his men recaptured the stolen property of Breadalbane and drove the cattle safely back. The respect he gained from this exploit resulted in other landowners seeking his protection.

However, not all the wealthy landowners in the area thought it necessary to pay 'blackmail' to ensure their cattle went unmolested while on the road to local markets. The Livingstons, for instance, an ancient family and Earls of Callander and Linlithgow, were not only wealthy but politically active on the Government side. In the early autumn of 1691, they were moving 200 head of cattle to the Michaelmas tryst at Stirling. The occasion proved irresistible to Rob and his clansmen in the Watch. Not only could they profit from the animals, but also strike a blow for the Jacobite cause.

Rob made plans accordingly. The road to Stirling in those days wound its way round the edges of the marshy wilderness of Flanders Moss by way of Kippen and Buchlyvie. His intention was to separate the cattle from the accompanying drovers as the herd passed through Buchlyvie. He posted men around the

the exceptionally long arms of Rob Roy (and his statue in Stirling shows this). Some have gone so far as to say he could tie his garters without bending from an upright position – a fact that sounds very like pure Gaelic colourful exaggeration. Whatever the length of his arms, he developed the very highest skills with the broadsword.

Just as important was his training in hillcraft – developing skills in tracking and hunting only attainable if the native is completely in tune with his environment in a sense now lost to urban man. As

Rob Roy's 'Watch' operated as far north as Loch Tay, shown here.

village, much to the inhabitants' disquiet and waited in the early morning for further action. As the day wore on, the villagers' state of alarm increased. The well-armed Highlanders loitering in their midst soon caused anxious messages to be passed to the neighbouring communities of Kippen and Balfron for support to rid Buchlyvie of these interlopers. And all the time, nothing was seen of the cattle. By the afternoon Rob realised that the men of all three communities had armed themselves with agricultural implements as makeshift weapons and were gathered threateningly on the edge of Kippen. Rob, having no quarrel with innocent villagers, moved his men out to the windy

On the famous occasion of the recovery of Breadalbane's cattle, Rob and his band pursued the raiders across the Moor of Rannoch.

Kippen – scene of the raid by Rob that alarmed the authorities.

spaces of Kippen Muir, which still gave a suitable vantage point to watch for the approaching herd.

Then, late in the afternoon, several events seemed to happen at once. The cattle appeared, Rob moved to intercept, but the villagers, perhaps seeing the movement as threatening their homes, came down on the Macgregors to block their path. Conflict seemed unavoidable and Rob ordered his men to attack, using only the flat of their broadswords – these were, after all, his own countrymen, who had mistakenly become involved. However, their spirited resistance was so intense that serious measures had soon to be adopted to prevent the cattle from passing on their way unscathed. The cudgels and sickels of the villagers fell back before the sharp edge of deftly handled steel. Then the drover was cut down and the cattle taken.

The involvement of the villagers in a business which did not concern them had so exasperated Rob that, after ensuring that the Livingstons' herd was safely escorted back to his territory, he made his way to Kippen to reason with the villagers. Finding that all had fled he helped himself to the villagers' cattle too, driving these in a second herd back to the wild landscape of the Trossachs.

The whole affair was talked of for years after and made a strong impression on the minds of the Government Ministers, reminding them that the Highlands were not as yet under the Government army's control.

By the early 1690s Rob was thus involved with legitimate cattle-dealing, the almost legitimate protection activities of the Watch and, finally, with cattle-reiving which (in Lowland eyes) was inexcusable – even if there were plenty of Jacobites north of the Highland line who would have been delighted at the embarrassment and loss of face which Rob's activities caused to the wealthy 'Whigs', as the Government supporters were known.

In spite of this hectic life, he found time to marry Mary of Comar. Helen Mary Macgregor came from within the clan, from a farm on the east side of Ben Lomond. Their new home was to be at Portnellan on the north shore of Loch Katrine, not far from Glengyle itself where he had grown up. Now, Rob's activities, legal or otherwise, had inevitably resulted in a high standing in the Clan Gregor. He was not Chief, as at this time his cousin, Archibald of Kilmanan, had inherited the title. But Archibald knew that the young Rob's exceptional talents and energies could serve the clan well and, accordingly, provided land for him at Inversnaid on the shores of Loch Lomond. His new house was built there and in the next few years his landholding was to expand greatly in this area until by the turn of the century he was to own a swathe of land along the east bank of Loch Lomond, called 'Craigrostan'.

But the intervening years were far from easy. Many historians have described the harsh winters and poor

Portnellan on the banks of Loch Katrine. On this site was the house that Rob occupied after his marriage.

A romantic Victorian print of Loch Lomond.

summers that marked the end of the seventeenth century. Doubtless Rob and his branch of the clan had to resort to cattle-raiding in order to survive. By about 1700 the Macgregors virtually controlled the passes around the Trossachs area – certainly around Aberfoyle where the Highlands gave way to the lush Lowland pasture – as well as Glen Dochart, which to this day carries the main routes west towards Crianlarich. In Strathyre, too, where the glen opens out beyond Loch Lubnaig, no cattle would pass without the Macgregors' scouts obtaining intelligence of their owner and destination.

Legitimate droving would be expanded, for cattle played a major part in the export trade from Scotland – at least 30,000 head of cattle passed over the border each year. In the early years of the eighteenth century Rob would have recruited a highly trained body of clansmen skilled in hillcraft, tracking and speedily moving herds over difficult terrain. This intimate knowledge of the country plus efficient intelligence-gathering was to draw the attentions of

landowners nearby, powerful men in high Government office.

The final factor in the approaching crisis in the fortunes of Rob Roy Macgregor was simply the significant times in which he lived. Scotland stood on the brink of giving up her Parliament as she had given up her Crown over one hundred years before. Hostility between the two nations was still a possibility, especially if the Jacobite sympathisers could be roused. The English Parliament passed Acts concerning the succession of the Crown without consulting the Scots and then relations became worse when England banned the import of Scottish cattle – an act that bankrupted many a Scottish drover but proved equally hurtful to a nation that depended on salt beef to feed its armies. There was talk of war and help from France, where James Edward Stuart waited an opportunity. Out of these political complexities in a particularly stormy period was born the Union between the two countries.

Rob did not declare himself too openly against the prevailing political climate – perhaps preferring to build a sound

Loch Achray and Ben Venue in the heart of Rob Roy country.

business base and hope for better times. His near neighbour in the south was the Duke of Montrose, of the powerful Graham family that dominated the lands around the Lowland end of Loch Lomond. Eastwards were the lands of the Murrays; the family had been split by the Jacobite cause, yet the Duke of Atholl remained politically powerful. To the west, with their headquarters at Inveraray Castle, were the Campbells, with their centuries-long good fortune to be supporting the right Crown at the right time – Rob's mother was herself a Campbell. All these men were to play their part in a drama which was about to unfold.

Although politically in the opposite camp, James, the fourth Marquess and first Duke of Montrose, did not hesitate to become involved in business dealings with Rob, so great had his reputation for shrewd buying and selling and trustworthy negotiation become. The enormous sum of £1,000 was raised by Rob from Montrose in order to buy cattle for fattening in the Lowlands. Rob's trusted chief drover MacDonald was given the

bills of exchange in the spring of 1712 and sent off with assistance to bring in the animals. Rob was well accustomed to handling such large sums of money – and in an age when a man's word was security enough, he would have given little thought to the trust he had to show in his colleague.

But the huge sum proved too much of a temptation for MacDonald. He disappeared, after buying cattle on the bills of exchange and then reselling them. He was never to be seen again. Rob was now in a very difficult position. His own debtors owed him enough to cover the amount but understandably his first impulse was to take off in hot pursuit of MacDonald. This he did, with very little explanation to anyone. After a fruitless chase he then attempted to seek out his two principal debtors, who, not surprisingly, themselves vanished. But the worst aspect of all lay in the terms of the loan. Rob had set his property of Craigrostan as security and Montrose, on hearing of Rob's apparent disappearance, was about to take direct and ruthless action. The business community

Ben More and Strathfillan, scene of Rob Roy's revenge on a Campbell land agent.

in Edinburgh and Glasgow were aghast; rumours spread that Rob had seized the funds to support the arming of rebel Jacobites. The Edinburgh *Evening Courant* ran an advertisement for four days in June 1712, for the arrest of Rob Roy, significant for the fact that it carried no description of the man, so well known was he.

The mystery of this turning-point will never be solved. MacDonald never re-enters the story. But the deed had ruined Rob and the political overtones became clear when Rob received a communication from Montrose. It seemed that his wish was to use Rob as a political tool. Montrose feared greatly the return to politics of the Duke of Argyll following active war service abroad. The two families had been rivals for centuries. He needed some damning evidence against

his rivals and thought he could secure it by forcing Rob to swear that Argyll was in collusion with the Jacobites.

Rob refused to bear false witness. Montrose wreaked a terrible revenge. He sent his factor, Grahame of Killearn, to Rob's house at Craigrostan to evict Mary and the children. All stock and goods were seized and the family turned out into the bitter weather. All Rob's attempts to pay back the loan had been in vain. Montrose's true intentions were revealed. Though his plan to involve Macgregor had failed, he at least had added to his extensive landholdings. Rob was declared an outlaw; Mary and the children found shelter with her kinsfolk nearby, where Rob was reunited with them.

The imposing cone of Ben More rises steeply from the main road through Glen

Dochart, carrying visitors eager for the scenic delights of the far west. In many stretches it is a fast road and it is unlikely that visitors even glance at the ruined roofless dwelling standing above the road on a low shoulder of the mountain. Yet the ruin marks the spot of the original cottage that Rob and his family were given by the Earl of Breadalbane, one of the Campbell family, following the disastrous affair of the missing drover. Clearly the Campbells would be grateful for Rob's loyalty in refusing to implicate them in any Jacobite conspiracy – and doubly so as Breadalbane himself was a Jacobite sympathiser, so complicated was the political situation at this time.

A man of Rob's talents would prove useful on Campbell territory, where Montrose, in any event, would not dare to come in force. But the full implications soon dawned on Rob. At the age of forty-three he was now beyond the law, having lost all security and with the status of an outlaw. There was only one course open. Since the Grahams had ruined him, his revenge would be upon their lands. He quickly organised a network of sympathisers and soon cattle and grain were being lifted at dirk- and pistol-point from the steadings of the Grahams and their tenants. Gentlemanly extortion, too, was soon feared by the wealthier tenants of Montrose. Their rents were collected by Macgregor raiding-parties who always gave a signed receipt.

The humbler tenants themselves had little to fear and in a Robin Hood-like incident one tenant in the village of Balfron, who was about to be evicted for arrears of rent, appealed to Rob for assistance. Having ascertained which day had been fixed for the seizure of her possessions by the factor, Rob arrived early with enough money for the old cottar's debts to be paid in full. He instructed her to obtain a receipt from the factor, who duly arrived, relieved her of the money and was, naturally, ambushed by Rob's men on the way to Stirling in order for Rob to retrieve his funds. The factor was the same Grahame of Killearn who had evicted the Macgregor family.

Though Rob was nominally under the protection of Breadalbane, that he was still very much his own man is shown by the famous tale of his treatment of a Campbell land agent who had evicted a family of Macgregors living in another part of Glen Dochart. (With such a stormy history of proscription in law for

The River Dochart at Killin.

Tyndrum – once Campbell territory. Rob Roy lived eastwards at Auchinchisallen for a time.

Communal porridge bowl and a variety of knives and weapons, all from Glen Gyle House and dating from Rob's time. Rob himself is said to have used at least some of these artefacts.

a variety of misdemeanours, usually involving cattle, the clan was scattered in several parts of the southern Highlands.) Rob sent out a party of his followers to bring in the agent, though he was well within the Campbell territory farther to the west. They brought him before Rob at Tyndrum and 'persuaded' him to renew the Macgregor lease. It occurred to Rob that nearby was the Pool of St Fillan, which at this time was believed to have healing properties, particularly for lunacy. The Campbell man was given the 'treatment' – ducked in the pool, then dragged to the churchyard of St Fillan's Chapel and there tied to a wooden frame thoughtfully provided in order to carry out the curative rites on the infirm subjects. The theory was that the Saint himself appeared and loosened the bonds of those he considered to be cured. Whether this happened, or whether some passing traveller took pity on the cold wet agent has not been recorded.

But on the wider canvas of national affairs, the unstable politics continued. Queen Anne was paying Highland chiefs regular sums to ensure their co-operation and after her death the Crown passed to George I, who knew or cared little for Highland problems. Disenchanted Ministers cast about, testing for a Jacobite Rising that all seemed sure was imminent. Montrose had found himself high office as Secretary of State and his shrewd mind sensed the gathering storm. One event in particular troubled him – the Crieff tryst or autumn cattle sale, where Highland men would gather in large numbers.

When the great fair opened, troops and Montrose's spies were much in evidence. These were rough times – a group of MacDonalds cut off an exciseman's ear when he attempted to tax them for drinking whisky in public. Worse, Rob and thirty armed followers surrounded the market cross in the town centre at midnight, and loudly drank to the true King's health, referring to James in exile in France. This disturbance was to become the keynote of a well-nigh openly pronounced disenchantment with King George all over the country. Meanwhile, Rob and his men had dispersed before troops could move in.

Before long, the Earl of Mar had raised

Loch Lubnaig, scene of one of Rob's many escapes from Government forces.

As a Jacobite, Rob supported the Earl of Mar and the Raising of the Standard in rebellion in 1715, which is shown in this nineteenth-century print.

the Jacobite flag in Aberdeenshire and Rob was recruiting supporters. The commander of the Government forces in Scotland was John, the second Duke of Argyll, a formidable soldier. The rebels raided Montrose lands along Loch Lomond, but John of Argyll's experience and sure judgement prevented the capture of Edinburgh. As the autumn wore on doubts must have grown in Rob's mind about Mar's leadership.

Behind the ramparts of the Ochil Hills above Stirling, the slopes fall away more gently to Strathallan and the valley that leads to Perth. These high, open, windy moors were to be the scene of one of the oddest battles ever fought in Scotland's story; a battle that might have changed the course of British history – and one which Rob Roy would witness, though his own part would be small and late. It was November, the high ground of Sheriffmuir frosted and bleak. John of Argyll was at Stirling with an army half the size of the rebels. When the Duke brought his army out to meet Mar, Rob himself would have been elsewhere, on a reconnaissance of the Fords of Frew on the Forth some miles from the battle site.

The two armies faced each other, Argyll narrowly winning the race for the highest ground. In the ensuing clash each wing of the armies was to defeat the other in an indecisive mêlée that resulted in the uncertain Mar ordering a withdrawal and the shaken Argyll also falling back at nightfall. Both sides were to use the encounter as propaganda. A variety of writers would have Rob engaged in activities that ranged from plundering the dead of both sides to being an agent for Argyll all along. More importantly, the rebellion was all but over, though Rob was to fight actively in the east of the country before returning to his homelands. What he must have thought when the news was brought that James himself had landed is not recorded. The campaign had foundered and eventually the uncrowned James sailed to Europe and out of history.

All this time, Montrose still wished Argyll out of the way of his career and again offered Rob Roy his lands back if he

Stirling Castle, held by the Duke of Argyll for the Government in the 1715 uprising.

The Ochils today from Stirling Castle. The battle site at Sheriffmuir lies westwards.

Inveroran
Loch Tulla
Bridge of Orchy
Loch Lyon
LOCH ETIVE
A82
River Lochay
Glen Orchy
River Strae
Loch Lubhair
Loch Dochart
Tyndrum
Strath Fillan
Lochawe
A85
A85
A82
River Dochart
Crianlarich
A85
Glen Doch
BEN MORE
Lochea
LOCH AWE
Balquhidde
ROB ROY'S GRAVE
SITE OF ROB ROY'S HOUSE
A819
Loch
River Shira
Glen Shira
River Fyne
A82
Loch Doine
Strat
Ardlui
A83
Loch Stay
Portnellan
INVERARAY CASTLE
ROB ROY'S CAVE
Inversnaid
Inveraray
A815
Loch Katrine
Loch Arklet
A83
LOCH FYNE
Tarbet
THE TROSSACHS
Arrochar
Loch Chon
Lochgoilhead
B829
Loch Ard
Aberfoy
Iverbeg
Rowardennan
Loch Goil
LOCH LONG
Glen Mallan
Loch Eck
A815
Luss
Buch
Garelochhead
Balmaha
A814
B837
LOCH LOMOND
Drymen
Ardentinny
Shandon
A82
Rhu
A811
Strath Blan
Blane Water
Clynder
Rosneath
Helensburgh
Kilmun
Balloch
Holy Loch
Cove
Rosneath Point
Jamestown
A809
Sandbank
Kilcreggan
Alexandria
Bonhill
Gourock
Dunoon
TO GLASGOW
Renton
GREENOCK
DUMBARTON
LOCH STRIVEN
A815
RIVER CLYDE
A82
A8
PORT GLASGOW
Duntocher

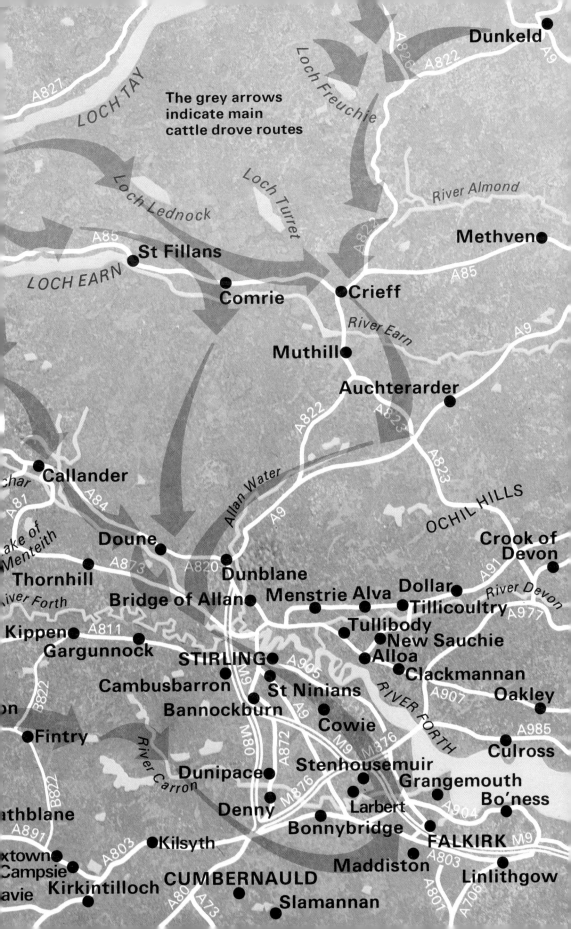

The grey arrows
indicate main
cattle drove routes

LOCH TAY

A827

Loch Freuchie

Dunkeld

A826

A822

A9

River Almond

Loch Lednock

Loch Turret

Loch Earn

A85

St Fillans

Comrie

Crieff

Methven

A85

A9

LOCH EARN

River Earn

Muthill

Auchterarder

A822

A823

A823

Allan Water

OCHIL HILLS

Callander

A81

A84

Doune

A820

Dunblane

Crook of
Devon

A91

River Devon

A977

Thornhill

Lake of
Menteith

A873

Bridge of Allan

Menstrie Alva

Dollar

Tillicoultry

River Forth

Kippen

A811

Gargunnock

Tullibody

New Sauchie

STIRLING

Alloa

Clackmannan

Oakley

A907

Cambusbarron

St Ninians

Bannockburn

A905

A9

RIVER FORTH

B822

Fintry

River Carron

Cowie

Culross

A985

M9

M80

A872

M876

Dunipace

Stenhousemuir

Grangemouth

Bo'ness

Denny

Larbert

Bonnybridge

FALKIRK

M9

A904

athblane

A891

B822

A803

Kilsyth

Maddiston

Linlithgow

xtown

Campsie

avie

Kirkintilloch

CUMBERNAULD

Slamannan

A80

A73

A801

A803

A706

Inveraray Castle. Rob and his men surrendered to the Duke of Argyll on this site.

would implicate Argyll in any Jacobite dealings. Rob not only refused, but continued his raids on Montrose territory. A desperate chapter in Rob's life was about to start.

The first sign of this must have been the sound of a bolt being drawn on the door of the change-house at Crianlarich. Montrose had called in the navy to land troops at Dumbarton. The Militia had learned of Rob's whereabouts and had surrounded him as he slept. Even Grahame of Killearn, Montrose's factor, was there. But the door was small and only permitted a single person at a time to enter. Soon it was piled with the soldiers cut down by the Highland blade. Then the change-house main doors were burst asunder by the Macgregors as they rushed for freedom. They drove back the Militia and escaped, though not before bringing down more soldiers with flint-lock and broadsword.

Parliament passed an Act containing the names of all those accused of treason in the 1715 Rising – and Rob's name was on it. This was all the justification needed for a high-profile military presence in the Highlands with General William Cadogan commanding. Rob knew that Breadalbane lands would be raided. Troops did take over Finlarig Castle – the same place that had seen Rob's triumphant return with Breadalbane's cattle a whole lifetime before – and, the worst news of all, a company of Swiss mercenaries was marching along Glen Dochart towards Rob's home at Auchinchisallen. He planned an ambush but the sheer numbers prevented effective action. After an exchange of fire that felled several soldiers, his band retreated southwards among the high hills around Ben More.

Still Montrose pursued his campaign against his rival Argyll and looked for evidence from Rob – little understanding the Highland code that hated treachery, false witness and the underhand dealing that had raised many a Lowland noble to high office. Even with the promised rewards from Montrose and the machinations of his law agents who acted as go-betweens, Rob would not commit perjury or involve himself in any way with a Lowland justice that he considered to be debased. Under the constant pressure from Montrose, Rob had only one person in authority to whom he could turn – Argyll himself. He surrendered along with many of his band, handing over their weapons to Argyll's men – but not before ensuring that the arms given up were the rustiest and most unserviceable that they possessed!

It might be surprising to learn that a clan who had taken the Government side should now be seen to be harbouring a known outlaw. Perhaps it was Argyll's admiration for the true Highland spirit, perhaps also that Rob had Campbell connections on his mother's side, that ensured he was well treated. Finally the Duke himself would doubtless be grateful that Rob had revealed to him the intentions of Montrose in the political arena. Although in comparative safety at Inveraray, the Campbell headquarters, in spite of receiving protection from the

John Campbell, second Duke of Argyll, under whose protection Rob lived. Painting by William Aikman, by courtesy of the National Galleries of Scotland, Edinburgh.

clan in writing, Rob was still in great danger farther east in his Trossachs homeland. At this time, he built a house in Glen Shira beyond Inveraray, deep in Campbell territory. The ruined walls are today still evident. But he was to use this

Early prints of the Highlands were more concerned with atmosphere than geographical accuracy, as in this example of the Highlands from below Callander.

base only infrequently, preferring to return to his home in the Trossachs, to be with Mary and the children.

Now he was escorted everywhere by a hand-picked company, even, it is said, wearing a steel plate below his bonnet. With the winter of 1716 approaching he needed a spectacular success in his continued vendetta against Montrose, to enable some degree of winter comfort. He knew that November was the month in which the Montrose tenants paid their rent. His plan was to secure some of those funds for his own use. As it turned out, once again, Grahame of Killearn, Montrose's trusty factor, was to face Rob, this time down the barrel of a cocked pistol.

At the Inn at Chapelarroch, where the Drymen to Gartmore road crosses the Kelty Water, Rob and his band calmly walked in on Grahame busily counting the money. Rob counted out an appropriate sum for himself, rewrote receipts for the tenants, ordered Grahame to write his own ransom note and bundled money and factor off to Loch Katrine.

Rob had miscalculated on one point only. So stung was Montrose, that no ransom funds were forthcoming – instead, the Duke used his influence to rouse attention to Rob in military circles. There was talk of building a barracks at Inversnaid with the express intention of quelling this troublesome band for good.

Rob Roy country today is popular with tourists, shown here fishing the River Teith in the Pass of Leny.

At the better-known eastern end of Loch Katrine is the Sir Walter Scott *steamer departure point.*

Meanwhile Rob, for all his ruthless reputation, allowed Grahame to go unharmed, even returning his accounts books, clearly not wishing to inflict repetitive paperwork on even his worst enemies! When the factor reported to Montrose – having walked from the outskirts of Glasgow, where he was released, to the town centre where Montrose now lived – he could give no unfavourable report on how he was treated, while in the custody of Rob. No doubt, this comment made Montrose even angrier.

He wanted action from a military command that was unwilling to send its troops into the winter hills against the well-trained guerrillas, as the Macgregors must be considered. Plans for the barracks at Inversnaid went ahead and even the King himself supported Montrose. In the spring of the year an expedition was planned, arms stocks were moved to headquarters at Buchanan House and from there distributed to tenants near by – but before the organisation and muster was complete, Rob was down from the hills. With his band he quickly raided each arms cache in a lightning strike that resulted in the

Macgregors holed up once again in the Loch Katrine area, before the military could act.

To the tenants in this 'buffer zone' on the edge of the Highlands it must have been a great talking-point, how the might of the Grahams could not bring in the elusive Macgregor, even with the support of the civil authorities. All the ingredients of the folk hero were there. But Montrose secured the legal right to raise a company against these robbers, in a carefully worded document designed to ensure that his company was free to attack any clan that was under the slightest suspicion of involvement with the Macgregors. The net was closing. Montrose himself entered the battle.

On hearing rumours that Rob was in the Lochearnhead area, the expedition with Montrose at its head, set off northwards, over the hill road from Aberfoyle. After a foray up Loch Katrine, the very heart of the Macgregor territory, they skirted below the outcrop of Ben A'an that guards the pass to the loch and by way of Loch Lubnaig, north of Callander, they reached Strathyre. There, the company learned that Rob had most recently passed through and was

Aberfoyle, on the very edge of the Highlands.

Lochearnhead, north of Balquhidder Glen.

Callander, with Ben Ledi guarding the main route northwards.

said to be resting in Balquhidder, only a short way ahead.

With a carefully chosen band, Montrose made with all speed northwards. At dawn, the cottage in which Rob had spent the night was surrounded. He was still asleep when he was confronted, his sword lying in a corner of the room. He was bound with a leather belt, mounted and led in triumph towards Stirling. Accounts differ in detail over the next development. One of Montrose's tenants, some say, who was in the company that guarded Rob, owed him some service for past favours. As the troop was approaching the Fords of Frew, so dangerous was

Rob made his daring escape while crossing the Fords of Frew.

the state of the water that the order was given to untie the captive, and to remount him, secured to one of the escorts. By chance, it was James Stewart, this same tenant. Perhaps Rob had to persuade or threaten him to assist. Somehow, he still had concealed a small knife. The waters at the fording were swollen and icy and night had fallen. As the doubly-laden horse stumbled and splashed, Rob cut himself from Stewart, dropped from the saddle and plunged into the foaming water. With supreme presence of mind he released his plaid. In the gloom, this dark, floating shape drew the gunfire and swordthrust, and in the resulting confusion Rob swam to safety. Sadly, history records that so furious was Montrose with Stewart that he struck him such a blow with his pistol butt on gaining the bank, that the tenant was permanently brain-damaged.

But this blow was the last to be struck even indirectly against Rob Roy by Montrose. The Duke confessed himself beaten.

However, once again Rob was to attract attention from men of high office who wished to use him for political ends. The Duke of Atholl of the Murray family had his headquarters at Blair Castle. He was now to play an important part in Rob's next series of adventures. His two sons had joined the Jacobite forces during the Rising of 1715. He himself had not done so, but at Court there was still the suspicion or taint of Jacobitism and the Duke needed some demonstration that he was a loyal Hanoverian. The bringing-in of Rob Roy was deemed a worthy target of his vast resources. But having seen Montrose fail by armed means, Atholl tried other tactics – simple treachery.

His son was sent with letters to Rob, requesting that he meet the Duke to discuss political affairs and most earnestly granting him safe-conduct. The meeting was arranged at Dunkeld House. Rob responded with enthusiasm to the request. He had spared Atholl lands even in his most desperate days. Contemporary readers might find this trust surprising, considering that Rob was to meet, in effect, a representative of the Government that had been trying to capture him – but in the moral code of the Gael, a man's word was his bond and would be trusted absolutely.

At the meeting, Rob must have listened with growing incredulity, as well as a fearful apprehension, as Atholl proposed that Rob give evidence of the Jacobite dealings of the third powerful duke – Argyll, himself. The motives of John Murray, first Duke of Atholl had turned out to be no different from Montrose's. Rob was seen only in terms of the assistance he could give for political advancement. That Rob would be able to

co-operate only by treacherous lying was a notion, which, if it crossed their minds at all, was of no consequence. Was he not, after all, only a common robber?

Rob was alone, and weaponless. Atholl called for his armed retainers when he realised that Rob was not going to co-operate. The Highlander had assumed he was to be discussing his submission to the House of Atholl. Instead he was led, heavily escorted, into imprisonment at Logierait Castle, six miles from Dunkeld. Flushed with his triumph, Atholl wrote to the King. But Rob had friends and clansmen who knew of the circumstances of his imprisonment. Even more signifi-

Blair Castle, home of the Duke of Atholl.

Dunkeld – near here Rob met with the Duke of Atholl.

cantly, there is a suspicion that the Atholl family were certainly not of one mind in the taking of Rob Roy. Within a day of his arrival at Logierait he had made friends with his guards, who were doubtless flattered by the attentions of this celebrity. He was allowed to receive a quantity of whisky from his kinsmen. He liberally shared this out, even gaining the consent of Atholl's son Lord Edward Murray to have his bonds removed.

Such was the personality of Rob that his guards were sufficiently relaxed after a very short time, with the whisky and the tales that Rob had to tell, to see nothing suspicious in the arrival of Rob's ghillie and a horse. The servant came bearing tales of how Mary, Rob's wife, was anxious – which was hardly surprising in the circumstances. The sympathetic head gaoler readily gave permission for Rob to write a note to Mary. Perhaps the whisky had dulled the wits of the guards as Rob went to the door with a gaoler to hand over the note. He greeted the servant, hesitated as if wishing to say more, and closed the gap between himself and the horse as he exchanged a few words. Suddenly, the reins were thrown in his hands and he was off, before the befuddled guards could focus or reach for their muskets.

Atholl was made a laughing-stock and must have bitterly regretted so prematurely writing to the King. But he was a man of action, too, and had soon organised a party to track Rob down. He had underestimated, as all the others did, the depth of sympathy for Rob, even among the Murrays, the Duke's own people. No one would betray his hiding-place, though the anxieties and hardships had by now laid Rob low with a fever. He was cared for in Balquhidder. Very soon after, Rob managed to summon enough energy to condemn his enemies in writing and had the document printed and distributed. Montrose and Atholl, in particular, would have found it decidedly unflattering.

In fact, an odd liaison developed between the rivals at this point, so intense grew their hatred of Rob Roy Macgregor. Atholl's Chamberlain, Donald Stewart, was dispatched to assist Montrose. On the road from Blair Atholl to Buchanan House near Loch Lomond, he met Grahame of Killearn, the same trusty factor who, while in the service of Montrose, must have found Rob Roy an occupational hazard, so often did he encounter him and come off worst. The two right-hand men of the Dukes discussed plans for the outwitting of the Macgregor. As it chanced they met late in the day and nightfall overtook them in the near vicinity of Loch Katrine. The territory was more familiar to Montrose's man than Atholl's, but nevertheless they found a cave nearby in which to spend the night. Dispatching their only servant to find wood for a fire, they decided to wait till morning before attempting to link up with the other Montrose scouts who were scouring the area.

The comic incident that follows has, no doubt, been embellished in the telling by many writers, but incredibly, it seems that they had chosen to spend the night in the very cave in which Rob had already hidden himself, having noted the numbers of Militia in the vicinity. The servant had returned and the fire had been lit when the three men were startled by stirrings from the gloomy recesses of their shelter. Fully armed, Rob himself stepped into the firelight. Killearn recognised him instantly, as did the servant, and stumbled out of the cave in an undignified retreat, hastened by Rob firing his pistol to further alarm them. The words that he then exchanged with Atholl's Chamberlain can be imagined – as presumably the man now realised that he was alone and unarmed in the presence of his master's sworn enemy. But Rob let him go, after reminding him that armed Macgregors were also in the glen and that these incursions ran serious risks.

Though sparing the lives of the Dukes' followers Rob was not left in peace. In a final desperate strike, Atholl obtained Government cavalry and in a lightning raid which travelled faster than Rob's scouts he laid hold of Rob himself while at Monachyle Tuarach, his cousin's farm in Balquhidder Glen. The troop fled southwards with their quarry in case the Macgregors would attempt a rescue. Stirling was their destination as they took the road down Loch Lubnaig. It requires a feat of the imagination to imagine road links in those days – narrow twisty paths through oak woods and birch scrub, offering several opportunities for concealment. At a particularly steep stretch of hillside, somewhere near St Bride's Chapel, the cavalry horses were in some difficulty. There was deep water below, trailing branches above and soldiers cursing their mounts. Rob took his gamble at the narrowest point. He slipped from the saddle, scaring his own mount forward into the group in front. A shying animal immediately behind ensured that all was confusion. With troopers still fumbling for powder and shot, the muted colours of his plaid would have faded into the shadows within moments.

With this escapade in mind, military advisers at last realised that they dare not risk further failure for fear of encouraging other Highland chiefs to take up arms in revolt. This was, after all, still more than twenty-five years before the flame of Jacobitism was finally to be extinguished. Rob had significantly proved that a highly trained band, operating in mountainous territory with which it was familiar and in which it could count on the support of the local population, could easily outwit pursuing Government troops for considerable lengths of time. It was a lesson that has been demonstrated in modern warfare several times over – and these events took place long before speedy communications or radio had been invented. Thus it was possible for Rob to exist as a free man while, in modern terms for measuring distance, his enemies were close by.

Rob was by now approaching the age of fifty. He cautiously re-established himself among his own folk, obtaining land

Eilean Donan Castle was captured by Jacobite supporters in the ill-fated 1719 rebellion.

Glen Shiel, where Rob and the rebels were soundly defeated by superior Government fire-power in 1719.

near the head of Balquhidder Glen. This seemed to be a safe distance away from the new barracks at Inversnaid which, in the meantime, Montrose had built. (During its construction unidentified armed Highlanders had captured the workforce, later releasing them in the Lowlands which delayed progress for a whole season. This action was Clan Gregor showing its outrage at the building of this potential curb on their activities. In some ways, though, the building of the barracks may have helped matters, as the Government, Montrose and other parties anxious for peace in the Highland area at least felt they had done something constructive.) Perhaps Rob had by now other priorities, such as building up the business in cattle that had been so spectacularly interrupted some years before.

But he was not allowed to fade into the hills. It was 1719 and again Rob was to be briefly caught up in larger events. Jacobites were plotting abroad and England was at war with Spain. When asked to fight for the cause by Lord George Murray, Rob could hardly ignore the assistance so recently given by the Jacobite element in the House of Murray. Logierait Castle and the subsequent staunch support from the Murray clan put Rob in their debt. Thus while on the international front the Duke of Ormonde sailed for England with 5,000 Spaniards, the exiled Jacobite leaders sailed north to Scotland with a smaller company. The expedition was doomed by the time it landed. Doubt and uncertainty had besieged the clans in Scotland, though the Castle of Eilean Donan in Loch Alsh in the far west was in the hands of the rebels.

The last major military encounter in which Rob played a part took place a little to the east in Glen Shiel among the high mountains. His company of forty Macgregors found themselves on the side of a company of Spaniards, as well as MacKenzies, MacRaes, Maclennans, MacDougalls and Murrays. The company spread out over the flanks of a mountain that was subsequently to be known as 'Sgurr nan Spainteach' (Spaniards' Peak). Government fire-power, including mortar-bombing, dispersed

Balquhidder and Loch Voil, with the churchyard where Rob Roy was buried visible in the lower left of the picture.

the futile opposition. The Hanoverians again won the day and Rob Roy and his band retreated. The bolt-hole in Glen Shira was used again but finally Rob returned to Balquhidder, no doubt hoping that the authorities would not learn of his involvement in the hopeless affair. He had probably also heard the news that a storm had wrecked the main fleet off Cape Finisterre even before a shot was fired in Glen Shiel.

A year or two afterwards, the famous General Wade was put in charge of the army in Scotland. Rob's status in the land was high, partly helped by the publication of *The Adventures of a Highland Rogue* at this time. This greatly exaggerated tale of Highland adventures had made his name known throughout the land. The time was right for the final reconciliation with all parties. Argyll himself did the arranging, for Rob would trust him. Along with Montrose the three parties met together – somewhere – as no two writers give the same location. Rob was persuaded to petition General Wade in order to receive the King's Pardon and stormy events seemed to be drawing to a close.

Not that Rob ever sunk into totally law-abiding habits – in Lowland eyes. He still maintained a band of followers as a Lowland Watch – but now men who reared cattle were only too keen to pay for his protection. He was still the best drover in the country and his services were much in demand. This continued throughout the 1720s, bringing a measure of prosperity to his Balquhidder home. Naturally, in his last years, he relaxed his self-imposed task of collecting blackmail; besides, the Government had even given approval of a Watch operated by another Macgregor.

Among his neighbours were the MacLarens. There had been a dispute over rights to rent land in Balquhidder some short while before. Rob had to offer single combat to avoid bloodshed when the MacLarens marched in force to settle the dispute. The young Champion of the MacLarens had drawn blood, which no one had done before. It was a stern reminder to Rob that his powers were at last diminishing. Honour was satisfied for all parties, though, and the dispute settled. Now some months later, the leader of the MacLarens asked permission to visit Rob. It was early winter and the light was fading. Rob had been ill. Nevertheless, he requested Mary to draw his plaid about him and dress him with pistol and dirk before he met MacLaren, who had come to express hopes for peaceful co-operation in the coming year.

After the visitor left, Rob was exhausted. He said 'Now all is over. Put me to bed. Call the Piper. Let him play "Cha till mi tuille", for my time is come.' As the piper played the old lament 'I shall return no more', Rob Roy died at Balquhidder among his own people.

Rob Roy's grave in Balquhidder churchyard.

Ashet showing the Arms of a Chief of Clan Gregor.

ROB ROY

1671 Born at Glengyle, Loch Katrine.

1689 Battle of Killiecrankie, in which the Macgregors took the Jacobite side.

1689 Rob Roy's father captured while raiding cattle.

1690 Rob Roy's first exploit – the recovery of Breadalbane's cattle stolen by the MacRaes.

1691 The 'hership' of Kippen – a successful cattle raid that increased Rob's notoriety.

1693 Rob marries Mary of Comar. Builds house at Inversnaid.

1696–99 Succession of severe winters. Cattle-raiding increases.

1700–11 Expansion of Rob's cattle-dealing – an interval of comparative prosperity, although politically an unstable period. (Union of Parliaments in 1707.)

1712 Rob's chief drover absconds with the Duke of Montrose's capital for joint business venture. Rob declared bankrupt.

1713 Rob Roy declared an outlaw. Family evicted from Inversnaid home.

1714 Rob living at Auchinchisallen in Glen Dochart, under Breadalbane's protection.

1715 Rob Roy takes part in the Jacobite Rising and Battle of Sheriffmuir.

1716 Auchinchisallen burned by Government troops; hunt for Rob Roy stepped up; Rob gains protection of Campbells at Inveraray and builds house in Glen Shira. Rob takes Montrose's factor hostage and increases frequency of raiding against Montrose territories.

1717 Rob captured at Balquhidder – escapes while fording River Forth. Rob attempts negotiation with Duke of Atholl – captured again but escapes from Logierait Castle. Captured and escapes for a third time *en route* for Stirling Castle.

1718 Inversnaid Barracks built.

1719 Rob takes part in Glen Shiel Rising.

1720 Settles peacefully in Balquhidder.

1725 Formal pardon arranged through General Wade. Rob resumes cattle-dealing and cattle-protection schemes.

1734 (December) Dies at Balquhidder.